Negotiation Techniques

Start Succeeding Today

Preface

This book: *"Negotiation Techniques: Start Succeeding Today"* is intended for people who want to optimize their negotiating skills by using tried and tested negotiation techniques.

A number of individuals may assume that negotiating is easy; however, this is not entirely true. Anyone can try to negotiate; but not all people truly succeed in the end. This book will present simple but effective steps in negotiating effectively and successfully.

In addition, numerous examples are presented to allow you to understand the concepts more. Learning exactly how, when, and where to do it, will boost your success on the negotiation table.

Continue reading and you will soon benefit tremendously when you use the methods in your career, social, and personal life.

Thanks again for downloading this book. Have fun reading and learning!

Copyright © 2017 by R. Davis All Right Reserved.

No part of this publication may be reproduced, distributed, or transmitted in any form or by any means, including photocopying, recording, or other electronic or mechanical methods, or by any information storage and retrieval system without the prior written permission of the publisher, except in the case of very brief quotations embodied in critical reviews and certain other noncommercial uses permitted by copyright law.

Table of content

Contents

Negotiation Techniques 1

Start Succeeding Today 1

Preface 2

Chapter 1: Introduction to Negotiation Techniques 6

Chapter 2: Key Factors for a Successful Negotiation 9

Chapter 3: Skills You Must Hone As an Effective Negotiator 13

Chapter 4: The Basic Steps of Negotiation 20

Chapter 5: Talk Less, Listen More 27

Chapter 6: How to Be Bold During Negotiations 30

Chapter 7: Never Accept First Offers 33

Chapter 8: Pros and Cons of Initiating the First Offer 35

Chapter 9: Negotiation Techniques for Buyers-Sellers 38

Chapter 10: How to Remain Ethical throughout the Process 41

Chapter 11: Negotiating with Your Boss 46

Chapter 12: Negotiating with a Business Partner 50

Chapter 13: Negotiating with Multiple Groups 53

Chapter 14: Negotiating with Your Kids 56

Chapter 15: Controlling Your Emotions 62

Chapter 16: Handling Problems during Negotiations 65

Chapter 17: Examples of Negotiation Conversations 68

Chapter 18: Expressions/Statements that Excellent Negotiators Use 73

Chapter 19: Handling Objections in Negotiations 76

Chapter 20: Tips to Remember When Negotiating 81
Conclusion 85

Chapter 1: Introduction to Negotiation Techniques

Negotiation is a skill and an art. Whatever career or profession you are in, having the ability to negotiate well is one of the most significant skills you can possess. Why? Because you can use your negotiation skills in almost anything you do: applying for a job, asking for a raise, advertising your services, selling your goods, dealing with the people in your community and maintaining a healthy and fruitful relationship with your loved ones and friends.

In this predominantly material world, everything is fair game. You can negotiate on almost anything. But how do people perceive negotiations? What is negotiation?

What is negotiation?

Negotiation is a process where two or more conflicting parties brainstorm to come up with an agreement or compromise that is beneficial to all parties concerned. Often, these parties have their own goals, concepts and requirements.

Traditionally, the term 'negotiation' connotes a negative meaning. To most individuals, when two groups 'negotiate', they have to compete against each other, and only one winner must emerge. This is a flawed perception.

For genuine success to occur, negotiations must be perceived as a 'cooperation' between groups to produce mutual benefits for all participants.

If you actively participate in a negotiation with this positive frame of mind, most likely, you will achieve your objectives. The specific steps on how to achieve this quest will be discussed in the succeeding chapters.

Types of Negotiations

Negotiations have several types. These types are typically classified according to the type of negotiator and the item or aspect that's under negotiation.

1. **Lose-lose negotiations**

   These negotiations are those in which both parties are expected to lose. An example is when negotiating a car accident. This is a case when both parties suffer physical injury and lose money – no one wins.

2. **Win-win negotiations**

   These are negotiations where both parties are willing to work together to come up with concessions that can benefit them. An example of this is a business or partnership negotiation. Win-win negotiations can easily turn adversarial when negotiators are inexperienced. So, tread carefully during this process. You cannot afford to acquire a bad reputation during your first negotiation.

3. **Win-lose negotiations (fixed-pie negotiation)**

   One party emerges as the winner and the other, the loser. The negotiating parties 'compete' to win most of the 'slices in the pie' because there is only one pie and the size of the pie is fixed and does not vary. This is seen in negotiations regarding games. This is commonly used with one-shot transactions. A number of negotiators choose to use the win-lose method, even in cases when a win-win strategy is possible. You will have to withdraw strategically from these types of transactions, if you're not ready to lose.

4. Bad faith negotiations

These are negotiations that are accomplished with one or both parties having no intention of adhering to the settlements discussed during the negotiation. An example of this is when groups negotiate to buy time; a rebel group pretending to negotiate, so they can have time to regroup.

5. Adversarial negotiations

These are negotiations where the negotiators are adversaries. It's highly competitive because both parties are out to 'fight it out' and inflict harm to the other party.

6. Multi-party negotiations

These are negotiations that have more than two participants. An example of this negotiation is the negotiation between two or more friendly countries.

7. Collaborative negotiations

Win-win negotiations are considered as collaborative negotiations because there is collaboration between the participants. These are negotiations that promote cooperation, rapport and uses persuasion techniques to arrive at a satisfactory agreement. An example is a business partnership, peer to peer product sales, and other friendly negotiations.

Chapter 2: Key Factors for a Successful Negotiation

Participating in a negotiation can be a Herculean task – IF you don't know exactly what you are expected to do. Before participating in a negotiation, you have to ascertain that all the key factors required in this activity exist. As a negotiator, you should also know how to drive a hard bargain. For successful and effective negotiations to occur between two or more parties, these key factors must be present.

1. **Willing and effective negotiators**

   A negotiation cannot succeed without willing and effective participants. All significant individuals playing a primary role in the activity must be eager and truly interested in the negotiation. When the negotiators are not focused and are just going through the motions half-heartedly, most likely, the collaboration would also be haphazardly accomplished.

2. **Freedom of expression (language comprehension)**

   There must be freedom of expression in which all the parties can understand each other clearly - meaning they speak the same language. Language barrier can be a humongous problem to overcome. In cases where the language is different, there must be a method devised to communicate clearly. This will enable groups to comprehend what each one is saying.

   This is one of the major reasons why some countries do not always cooperate with one other because of the language barrier.

There may be instances in which the language is the same but the meaning can be different. For example, the word "plane" can mean different things to various people. It can denote an airplane to a pilot; a flat land to a geologist; and a spiritual plane to a priest. In this case, a working definition must be created to define terms specifically used for the negotiation process.

3. **Appropriate venue**

   The ambiance of any event will definitely affect the process being conducted. This has been proven by various research studies undertaken by numerous organizations from all fields of endeavor. Certain studies conducted in the academe had proven that the venue is a significant part of learning.

   In the study "The Effect of Classroom Environment on Student Learning", conducted by Ryan Hannah of Western Michigan University concluded that "Overall, the classroom environment plays a crucial role in keeping students engaged and allowing them to be successful within the classroom."

   If you find the previous example not specific, let's talk about the Butterfly Effect postulated by Dr. Edward Lorenz.

   The Butterfly Effect indicates that seemingly trivial events, such as the flutter of the butterfly's wings, can create gigantic ramifications later on in a dynamic process. This Butterfly Effect can trigger larger unexpected consequences as the activity proceeds.

   Negotiations are considered as dynamic activities too, and as such, any minor factor, such as the venue of the negotiations, can cause large effects while the activity unfolds.

Therefore, all minor details must be considered crucial. The Butterfly effect does not refer only to the venue but also to the other key factors in this list.

4. Complete knowledge of what the negotiation is all about.

Participate in a negotiation – ONLY - if you have complete knowledge of what it is all about. If you don't, and you are tasked to join the table, you have to do your own research and learn the details of what you are expected to negotiate. You can benchmark to determine the norms in that particular area.

Doing a thorough research and gleaning all the vital information can grant you more leverage and power. With knowledge comes power, and this power will allow you to gain more concessions from the other party/parties

5. Specified short term and long term objectives

Setting objectives for your negotiations will serve as the blueprint for your success. What is your primary goal and what are your sub-goals? The ultimate goal and the alternative goals should be clearly defined. Up to what extent are you allowed to negotiate?

6. Alternative choices of actions

Alternative choices/goals must be prepared so that they can be utilized whenever necessary. We call these contingency plans.

7. Correct attitude

This is one of the key traits that negotiators must possess. When negotiators have a positive frame of mind, this will attract good vibes and will result in genuine cooperation between the negotiating parties. Remember, one of your targets is to maintain good relationship with the other party despite differences of opinions.

These are the key factors involved in negotiations. They are still other minor factors that will be discussed in the succeeding chapters.

Chapter 3: Skills You Must Hone As an Effective Negotiator

People negotiate every day, unconsciously or consciously. Whether you are haggling over the price of an item or asking for a raise from your boss; you are negotiating. However, no one is born a negotiator. Negotiating effectively is a skill that has to be honed over a period of time. If you want to become a skilled negotiator, here are essential skills that you have to develop first:

1. **Communication skills**

    Communication is the vital language of negotiations. It entails three aspects: the sender, the language and the receiver. Genuine communication only occurs when the sender uses the appropriate language for the receiver to understand the message.

    There is such a thing, as the "right word" said at the "right time" with the "right tone" of voice. An example is this: Shouting "Stay calm!" during a lecture when everyone is listening intently to the professor would surely cause a commotion. But when you shout the same words during a fire, it would appear 'natural'.

    When negotiating, learn how to say things correctly, appropriately and in a timely manner. You can apply these significant tips to get you through the activity:

    - *Read the other party's non-verbal cues.* Nonverbal cues are crucial in negotiations. Often, the truth about the other party's statement can be observed from his/her actions.

Examples of positive nonverbal actions are: smiling; arms are hanging comfortably on both sides; warm handshake; sparkling eyes that look straight at you.

Examples of negative nonverbal actions are: arms crossed across chest; unsmiling face; maintains distance as far away as possible; unfocused eyes; fidgets; and sits at the edge of his chair.

When you observe the negative nonverbal cues, the other party may become anxious, so you have to put him at ease. Smile and build rapport by talking in a well-modulated voice and ensuring that everyone is seated comfortably.

- *Allow the other participants to speak freely.* Allow each participant to put in his two cents' worth. As the cliché goes: "Two heads are better than one."

- *Don't interrupt when someone is speaking.* Follow the time limit specified in the ground rules. A timer can ensure that the time is correctly observed.

- *Use simple language to avoid ambiguity.* Don't try to impress by using highfalutin words. You are there to negotiate and not to flaunt your erudition. Hence, present your ideas in a concise manner.

- *Clarify statements by the other party by asking additional questions.* If you want to stress a point, you can eradicate ambiguity by asking follow-up questions.

Let's say you are buying a farmland in Wyoming, and the statement of the seller is this:

> *"We have to include the taxes in the computations."*

You have to clarify this statement properly, so you have to ask more questions:

> *"What type of taxes are these?"*

The seller will have to explain and state precisely what he means by 'taxes". Does it include the value added tax, or the real estate property tax? Or the land transfer tax? Which ones are included?

2. Listening skills

The skill of listening intently will enhance your negotiation skills. You must listen and understand what the speaker wants to communicate to you. Taking down notes and highlighting the main concepts by each speaker is a good practice. Conversely, listening solely would be the best method, providing you remember what you have heard without referring to your notes.

3. Problem solving skills

Problem solving skills are needed to be able to negotiate well. You should learn the ability to identify the main problem; to analyze the data already given; and to determine the method that can solve the problem. Approaching the problem using the mathematical approach will facilitate the process.

- Write down all given data
- Identify the problem
- Find a method that can connect the given data with the problem
- Solve the problem

- Double check your answer

4. Diplomacy skills

You will need diplomacy when negotiating. Your chances of success are significantly increased when you know how to be tactful and diplomatic. Diplomacy is defined by the dictionary as "the art of dealing with people in an effective manner." Again, take note that a negotiation is collaboration and not a competition. Being diplomatic can win you brownie points but not rudeness or tactlessness.

You can practice being tactful through your daily dealings with people around you. Be conscious of what you say and how you say it.

5. Skills on building rapport

Building rapport with your fellow negotiators promotes camaraderie and a relaxed atmosphere. Don't worry, with experience, you can acquire this skill. A comfortable ambiance will lead to successful outcomes.

6. Skills on the ability to stay calm

If you become angry, learn how to calm down.

Here's a simple calming method you can do subtly, whenever you feel piqued.

- Request for a 10-minute break.

- Go somewhere quiet or private that is not far from the venue.

- Sit down or lie down with your back straight but relaxed. If you can't find a proper area, you can just sit down on a chair and do it from there.

- Inhale deeply through your nose and hold your breath for 6 seconds. Feel how the air enters your body.

- Then exhale forcibly through your mouth. Feel how the air rushes out from your lungs.

- While performing this exercise, mentally instruct yourself to relax and be calm. You can close your eyes to feel the entry and exit of air through your respiratory organs. This will allow you to focus on your breathing.

- Do this until you can feel your body relax, and your anger has subsided.

- Another variation of this relaxing exercise is to stand up with your arms akimbo.

- Raise your body by raising your heels. As you raise your body, inhale deeply through your mouth. Hold that position for 6 seconds.

- Then slowly lower your body as you exhale forcibly through your mouth.

- Do this until you feel your muscles relax and your anger has subsided.

- If you don't have a private space, you can always use the comfort room. It will only take a few minute to perform this exercise.

Learn how to use this short breathing exercise in any activity that stresses you out and you will be surprised how useful it can be. It also helps maintain the acid-base balance in your system through proper respiration. This will keep you healthy.

7. Decision making skills

Decision-making skills are necessary to become an excellent negotiator. When you are caught in a bind, you must have the skill to decide correctly on the next best Alternative Course of Action (ACOA). You could also take into consideration your BATNAS.

Your ACOA, however, must have been prepared days before the negotiation. So, all you have to do is select the most suitable choice. You will have to create several ACOAs based on the minimum terms of your negotiation.

Learn how to identify your weaknesses and then eliminate them by doing the opposite. Turn your lemons into lemonades, so to speak. Here are examples of weaknesses that can be turned into strengths.

- **Inferiority complex** – this weakness can be turned into self-confidence by constant practice and self-affirmation. You have first to change the way you think about yourself. Think that every individual is unique with his own assets and liabilities. Count your blessings: you are not mentally retarded; you have a roof over your head; you have complete body parts; you eat three square meals a day – with snacks on the sides, and most of all – you are normal. All you have to do now is to develop your personality. Appreciate all these and believe in your capabilities. It will be a long, arduous battle, but you can do it with dedication and will power.

- **Fear of public speaking** – no one is born a great speaker. Outstanding speakers are harnessed through constant practice and commitment to their craft.

  Demosthenes, the famous Greek orator, had a childhood speech impediment; nonetheless, he was able to overcome this by facing his fear head-on. He had practiced endlessly to improve his diction and method of delivery. Reportedly, he had placed pebbles in his mouth and had orated in the seaside amidst the crashing waves and howling wind. Later on, he was recognized as the greatest orator of Ancient Greece. You can be like Demosthenes through constant practice and dedication.

- **Inability to decide promptly** – this is a negative trait that can be converted to a positive one. What you must do is to practice every chance you get, until you inculcate the trait in your system.

- **Lack of problem solving skills** – Fret not, skills can be acquired. With determination you can learn this skill. What you need is constant practice and exposure. Refer to chapter 3 for the steps in developing your skills.

The concept is to eschew all these weaknesses and turn them into strengths. It is not a trivial feat, but it can be done with enough will power.

Chapter 4: The Basic Steps of Negotiation

There are certain steps that you have to follow to negotiate effectively and successfully. They are presented here in the simplest terms so you can implement them properly. These steps may be utilized in negotiations between two companies or groups.

Step #1 – Learn everything about the negotiation

This means you have to do your homework and prepare. Do a thorough research about the other party, and what is involved in the negotiation. What would be their most probable offer? What leverage can you use with them? Peruse information about the 'object' of the negotiation. Why are you conducting the negotiation? What do you or your company want/s to achieve? Gather all information that would help you triumph in your endeavor. Always go to the negotiation table armed with all necessary information. Remember that knowledge is power.

Step #2 – Set your objectives/goals

Next, you have to set your objectives. Identify your main and sub goals. Decide the bottom line terms as well. If you cannot achieve your major objective, what are the minimum terms that you can negotiate on? When do you decide to walk away from the negotiation? You must be courageous to end the negotiation if none of your ACOAs are accepted. You may also want to consider the possible objectives of the other negotiating party or parties.

Step #3 - Plan your sequence of action

Write down how you plan to go about the negotiation. The sequence of action has to be SMART (Specific, Measurable, Attainable, Reliable and Time-Bound). An example is this:

1. Prepare and research
2. Present facts
3. Explain proposal
4. Justify proposal
5. Listen to the other party
6. Help each other to find a solution to the problem
7. Compromise
8. Come to an agreement and finalize it
9. Implement agreement

Step #4 - Establish the Ground Rules

Before the negotiation starts, it's important that you establish the ground rules. You may want to furnish the other parties with a copy. You can ask suggestions from them about any changes they would like to add. These ground rules must be accepted by all participating groups or individuals. Here are vital items that you can include:

- **Select the venue** according to the properties presented in **chapter 2**.

- **Specify the time and day**. Choose a time that is pre-approved by all participants. Morning hours are preferable and a day with a good weather is best. So, there should have been a previous consultation about the availability of the negotiators. This can be accomplished quickly through phone calls or video calls. Understandably if the person is nearby, you ought to do it in person.

- **Stipulate the time allotted for each step.** Of course, this is not written on stone. You can always be flexible and adjust the time, when extremely necessary. This is included so that time is not wasted with unnecessary detours.

- **Identify the delimitations and limitations of the negotiation.** The delimitation is the boundary of how far the negotiations can go, and its limitations are the parameters that prevent the negotiations from proceeding further. All of these have to be stated clearly in the ground rules.

- **Create a set of sanctions corresponding to violations.**

    Example:

    Unprofessional conduct:

    1st offense – oral reprimand with incident report accomplished by the violator.

    2nd offense - termination from the negotiating panel.

    Non-compliance of ground rules:

    1st offense – oral reprimand with incident report accomplished by the violator.

    2nd offense - termination from the negotiating panel.

    Deliberate misrepresentation of facts:

    1st offense – termination from the negotiating panel.

    > You can prepare a more detailed description of what encompasses unprofessional conduct as the need arises.

- **Create the working definition of terms.** What are the most likely terms that you will be using during the negotiation? These have to be defined according to their functions in the event. Present this to all participating groups for approval and suggestions. After approval, a copy must be furnished to all parties.

Examples of working definitions:

1. Negotiation – all activities occurring inside the venue. Talks held outside the venue are not valid.
2. Contract – a written and notarized legal document that is signed by all negotiators detailing the agreement entered into by Party A and Party B.
3. Party A – refers to the potential buyer, ___, (name of buyer)
4. Party B – refers to the legitimate seller, ____, (name of seller)

Step #5 – Start on mutually agreed points of negotiation

Obviously, introduction of the participants is required. A brief introduction by the negotiator stating his position and function in the company can make everyone comfortable. After the introductions, a designated person or the chairman may read the Ground Rules that was previously agreed on.

An example is stating a focal point that both parties acknowledge, such as the importance of having a standard price for similar products.

Step #6 – Let both parties present their cases

You can present first or let the other party do it. Present your proposal clearly to prevent misunderstandings. Be willing to answer questions. Depending on the situation and the type of negotiations, you may reveal some or all of the facts about your terms. Although it is great for negotiating parties to put all their cards on the table, it is wise to leave some room for bargaining.

An example is when you are negotiating for the price of a real estate you want to purchase; you can name a price below the seller's price and then gradually increase the amount until you reach the maximum price that you are capable of paying.

After your presentation, you should listen intently to the other group's objectives and jot salient points that you should consider when compromising. This step is not used for arguing but for data dissemination. This is where both negotiating parties present their positions and arguments in a non-argumentative way.

Step #7 – Negotiate

There are two conflicting thoughts on whether you should offer first or not. Some negotiating experts believed that giving the first offer will strengthen your position because you know exactly what you want. Some negotiators though, recommend that you can encourage the other party to provide the first offer because their offer may actually be better for you.

An example is when negotiating for the price of a second-hand car: you can wait for the seller to state his price and bargain from there.

Negotiate step by step, as you have planned. This will ensure that you don't commit mistakes. The negotiation must not be argumentative but should be explanatory. Members of each group have to state their own negotiating positions honestly and clearly.

Step #8 - Conclude or break the negotiation

After both sides have presented their recommendations and supported their proposals, you can determine if your objective is accomplished or not. If not, evaluate their alternative offers if these are included in your sub-goals. Be courageous to walk away, if you haven't accomplished any of your goals and sub-goals. Nevertheless, be ready to conclude the negotiation quickly when the terms of the other party are acceptable.

Step #9 – Accomplish proper documentation

After the groups come to a compromise, remember to require all participants to sign the documentation of the activity. This will serve as an evidence and record of what transpired during the negotiation.

Step #10 – Express appreciation for everyone's cooperation

It's tactful to express your appreciation for everyone's cooperation. You can never predict when the next negotiation would be. Hence, build business relationships as you go along.

These are the basic steps when negotiating. Of course, you can modify the steps for your activity as you deem fit. After all, a negotiation is a dynamic activity.

Post-negotiation activities

Your task is not finished yet after your successful negotiation. The hardest part is yet to come. What should you look into?

1. Follow-up the other party in the implementation of the agreement. Both of you must have a copy of the contract.

2. Check on your customer often, especially when it concerns the sale of services or products. You can gain a loyal customer if you truly care about how useful the product is for him.

3. Re-negotiate if both parties agreed to do so. This can happen when the previous negotiation was not fully understood.

4. Monitor the outcomes of the contract. Were the goals of both parties truly attained? This can be promptly checked by going over the contract.

5. Talk with the other party and ask directly whether the outcomes were truly met.

Concluding a negotiation successfully brings pride to a negotiator. Basked in your success but continue learning and improving yourself. There will always be room for improvement.

Chapter 5: Talk Less, Listen More

Studies have proven that people who talk less and listen more are considered as good conversationalists. For negotiations to succeed, you must have the skill to talk less and listen more. Here are pointers on how to do this.

Know how to ask open-ended questions

Most people would want to talk about themselves; "my family", "my pet", "my career", "my hobbies", and "my thoughts." Thus, if you want people to talk more, ask something about themselves. Ask open ended questions that are not answerable by short phrases, or by a simple 'yes' or 'no'.

Examples of open-ended questions are those that start with "why", "describe", "how" and "what".

> *"Why did you participate in this negotiation?"*

> *"How would this negotiation affect your company?"*

By asking open-ended questions, you are handing over the baton of control to the other party. This can become dangerous in cases that you don't know how to handle it. So, balance your open-ended questions with closed questions that need simple answers. Examples of closed questions are:

> *"Are you contented with the current state of affairs?"*

> *"Where do you live?"*

You can be a good listener by knowing how to shift from open to close questions to maintain balance. Your end goal is to allow the other party to talk. Through this method, you can delve deeper into the genuine thoughts of the other party.

Let the other party elucidate on his answer

This is most applicable when you encounter closed-mouth participants. An example is when you ask the closed question, "Are you contented with the current state of affairs?" The answer will most likely be "yes" or "no". But you can follow this up with an open question, "Why do you think so?"

This will encourage the person to talk more in order to explain his stand.

Clarify the other party's concepts

Another method of letting the other participants to speak is to clarify their concepts or ideas. The following are sample questions:

> *"You're saying that this is a harmful way of harnessing power because of carbon emissions? Can you go over it again?"*

> *"I understand where you're coming from but can you expound more on your suggestion."*

> *"So, you stated that this car has been used for only three months, do you have any evidence to prove this fact?"*

> *"I see. So, you're living in Reed Avenue. What do you think about the peace and order situation there?"*

Maintain eye contact

While the other person/party is speaking, maintain eye contact. Don't look somewhere else, fidget or toy with your hair.

React to the statements

The other party knows that you are listening through your body language. Nod your head when you agree with the statement, or you can shake your head unobtrusively. Nonetheless, a positive reaction (nodding of the head) will motivate him to talk more. Therefore, be receptive of the other party's thoughts.

Glean the main thought

As you listen, learn the skill of gleaning the main thought and writing a summary as your reference notes later on. These seemingly trivial things can be crucial as the negotiation proceeds.

With constant practice, you can become a good listener and an accomplished negotiator.

Chapter 6: How to Be Bold During Negotiations

There will be some phase in the negotiation that you have to step up and be bold. You should anticipate this and psyche yourself to respond boldly whenever needed.

So, how can you be bold during negotiations?

There are various instances when you have to be brave and step forward. One instance is when none of your ACOAs is accepted. You have to stand up and voice out your position. Boldness does not mean becoming physically aggressive though. Yelling or acquiring a combative attitude is not being bold or brave. Boldness can be demonstrated in innumerable and appropriate ways, such as the following:

1. **Volunteering to provide more information** on a major point that the opposite party cannot comprehend.

   If you are done talking, but the issue is still unclear to the other party, you must be bold enough to raise your hand and explain the misunderstanding.

2. **Correcting misinformation**

   When the other negotiating party presents a misinformation about a fact, don't feel daunted to correct it. You can do it privately not to embarrass the person, or you may call him out during the negotiation, depending on the type of error. You will have to decide spontaneously if ever this incident happens.

3. **Making the first offer**

As previously discussed, you can only make the first offer if you are confident enough to pull it through. This is a bold move because when you present the first offer, this action will add apprehension and tension to your participation in the proceedings. You will have to be on your toes at all times. Nevertheless, if you pull it through, you will be respected and admired, not only by your peers, but by your co-negotiators.

4. **Confronting an uncooperative negotiator.**

   Be bold enough to confront an uncooperative negotiator. Depending on the situation, you can do it privately, or right after the act is done. What is important is that the unpleasant behavior should be corrected before the negotiations could proceed. Inform the person that his behavior is disrupting a supposedly positive outcome of the negotiations. Be frank in a tactful manner. It's not what you say but how you say it. You can read more about proper communication in the previous chapters.

5. **Walking away when the terms are unacceptable.**

   You must have the courage to walk away when the final terms are unacceptable to you or your company. In this instance, walking away is not an act of cowardice but of bravery. There is no use agreeing to a proposal that awards you nothing. In the long run, there can be a hidden potential in your boldness. Next time the same party negotiates in the future, they will offer more acceptable terms.

There are countless incidents where you can be bold and courageous. Based on your moral compass, be bold to wage a war against devious or wrong methods. The cliché: "Evil proliferates because good men do nothing" is likewise applicable in negotiations. Be bold to speak out whenever you observe something unfair.

Chapter 7: Never Accept First Offers

First offers are almost always exaggerated – especially when these come to prices. They can be exceedingly high or low; the seller offers the ceiling price, while the buyer offers the lowest price. Whether you are the seller or the buyer, never accept first offers. Negotiate for the right price that is affordable for your pocket, or sell at the right price that can earn for you an acceptable profit.

Why you should never accept first offers:

1. First offers are just pivotal points for you to negotiate from. It's like a flexible tag price. No matter how low the price is, give it sometime before saying "yes".

2. Accepting first offers will depict a wrong impression. The other party may think that something is wrong, or that he has negotiated ineffectively.

3. You will not obtain the best price for the item. You can accept the third or fourth offer because this would be nearest the true value of the product.

4. First-offer prices are meant to be negotiated. Experienced negotiators know this fact. So, they don't grab immediately but wait it out, and present a counter offer.

5. The best concessions occur when you don't accept the first offer. The party with the first offer will tend to add more to satisfy the needs of the other.

6. First offers act as anchors for the negotiation. The final result usually results from that sphere of influence.

Who makes the first offer?

There are conflicting observations about who should make the first offer. Many negotiators opined that the negotiator who made the first offer generally ended up with the most fulfilled objectives.

On the other hand, several experts postulated that negotiators must not make the first offer because they are exposing their goals unnecessarily to the other party.

It is observed that most negotiators with the first offers are confident enough to obtain what they wanted. They tend to have control over the negotiations. So, if you are not that confident, don't attempt to make the first offer, if you don't know how to follow through. Nevertheless, do not forget this vital rule: "Never accept first offers."

Chapter 8: Pros and Cons of Initiating the First Offer

As previously mentioned, initiating the first offer can be stressful and unnerving to a newbie. Because of conflicting views, I have decided to present the pros and cons, so you can decide on your own whether to make the first offer or not.

Pros

1. The first offered number/price acts as the anchor for the succeeding offers. Research studies have proven that the negotiator who provided the first offer usually enjoys a negotiation advantage. The counter offers will most likely within the range of the first offer.

2. The party that presented its first offer will have to defend and justify the offer before the other negotiator. This will establish the fact that the offering party is in control of the negotiations.

3. The other party will have to recognize this control and a relationship advantage occurs, in favor of the party providing the first offer.

4. Some studies have proven that the negotiator who presented the first offer had better satisfaction in the outcomes from the negotiations, and had gained more concessions and better terms. The same studies arrived at a conclusion that first offers were most successful when the negotiator was well-informed about the negotiations and knew essential information about the other party.

    If you are not well equipped with the correct information and you know nothing about the other negotiating party, NEVER make the first offer. Making the first offer could be disastrous when you do not know how to manage it properly, and what the other party is aiming for.

Cons

1. The other negotiating party will have an idea of the range that you are targeting. Let's say you offered $150 for an item, this will reveal early on that the price range you're aiming for is not lower than $150. When the opposing party comes to learn about this, you will be left with little room to bargain. Who knows? The price he wants to offer may be lower than your target price of $150.

2. The opposing party can obtain critical information from your first offer. This would be easy for veteran negotiators. They could use it to manipulate you.

3. You will not be able to learn about the bargaining power of the other party.

How do you construct the first offer? Go over these tips and make use of them when you are tasked to craft the first offer. The example here is when negotiating for a particular commodity or service

Tips in constructing first offers

1. Don't be too zealous by offering a price that overshoots the target price of the other party. By doing this, you may prompt him to walk away from the negotiation. Based on current trends, and an educated guess of the party's target price, you can generate your first offer.

This is the reason why you must have reliable information about the other party.

2. Your first offer has to be around your target price too. Aside from your target price, you need to decide on a reservation price that would set the limits of your acceptable price.

3. Be aggressive. This does not mean that you can go to the extremes. Bear in mind that your over aggressiveness can drive away the other negotiators.

4. Be ready to concede and accept counter offers - if they are profitable.

When you are not able to provide the first offer, your counter offer must be similar to your planned first offer.

Chapter 9: Negotiation Techniques for Buyers-Sellers

Skilled negotiators had made use of innumerable tactics and techniques in negotiating. As they say, "there are several ways to skin a cat." You may want to learn some of these tried and tested methods that buyers and sellers use.

For Sellers

1. Have complete information about the products or services you are selling. Nothing discourages a prospective buyer more than a seller who doesn't know his products.

2. Explain to the buyer the importance of your product or services. Discuss the difference of your product from other brands

3. Keep an open line for the buyer to be able to contact you readily. Provide your buyer your cell phone or office number.

4. Follow-up every now and then the status of your customer's interest in your product or services.

5. Take note of the buyer's verbal and nonverbal cues. Act in view of these cues. Do you observe restlessness or anxiety? Do something to ease the buyer's behavior. You may offer him coffee or drinks to calm him down. He might not trust you, so provide evidences that you are what you claim to be. Show an ID or a certificate.

6. Make small talk. Talk about your hobbies and then ask him his. This can help eliminate his discomfort. You are

not there to win a negotiation, but you are there to explain why he must avail of your product or services.

7. Obtain all relevant information from your buyer. This will provide you a chance to keep in touch with him, and turn him into your loyal customer.

For buyers

1. Before buying, double check the product/services, to confirm that the specifications stated by the seller are true. Scrutinize the product and check for any defects.

2. You have the upper hand in this type of negotiation, so take advantage of that by demanding the best product/services.

3. Learn all about the seller; his reputation, business, his goals and values. You can negotiate more effectively when you know more about the seller

4. Negotiate only if the seller is honest with you. Who knows what he can fabricate? Avoid these types of sellers.

5. Let the seller know that you are willing to look somewhere else if your objective is not accomplished.

In the end, both buyer and seller must conclude the negotiation having a win-win outcome.

The steps in negotiating for buyers and sellers are the same as any negotiation. The difference is that you are selling or purchasing products or services.

Chapter 10: How to Remain Ethical throughout the Process

Sometimes, it can be a burden to remain ethical throughout the negotiating process. This most especially when the other parties are out to gain their own objectives by hook or by crook. However, truly successful negotiators are those who had maintained their integrity and sterling character despite shady deals that their contemporaries had spawned.

Why is there a need for ethics in negotiation?

Ethics is defined by the dictionary as a set of rules that defines good and bad behavior. In summary, it distinguishes which actions are bad or good. This is needed because ethics is essential in effective negotiations. An ethical negotiator with an excellent reputation will encourage the other party to offer more concessions because they know they are not being deceived.

But how can you maintain your ethics and values during negotiations? How can you compromise without going against your values? Here are pointers on how to do this.

1. **Negotiate ethically**

    For others to be ethical, you have to ethical yourself.

    That's why you have to negotiate ethically, even while striving to posit your objectives. Avoid committing these unethical actions:

    - Deliberate lying that can inflict significant harm the other party
    - Failure to correct a misapprehension by the other party
    - Illegal methods of acquiring information

- o Threatening the other party to obtain a leverage
- o Manipulating the emotions of the other party to gain an advantage

Albeit you are expected to find all means to succeed in negotiating for your own self-interest, you must always do it within the bounds of the law.

Some expert negotiators believe that bluffing is needed to attain their goals. They consider bluffing as the essence of bargaining. For a number of effective negotiators; however, bluffing and deception are not needed to negotiate successfully.

Once your method becomes illegal, you are deemed to damage your self-esteem, character and reputation. Eventually, people in your field will discover your deception and will refuse to negotiate with you. That would end your career as a negotiator. Your bad reputation will surely catch up with you eventually. Keep in mind that it takes years to build a good reputation, but only seconds to destroy it.

2. Be proactive and not reactive

When the other party acts unethically, act and do not react. Distance yourself away from their illegal actions. Do NOT commit an unethical act to get back at them.

Never allow another person's bad behavior to change your ethical or moral compass. Maintain your ethics and follow your plan of action. Do not deviate from your goals.

3. Legal and ethical may not always denote the same thing

An action may be legal but unethical. An example is when a lawyer defends a criminal that has confessed to him about his crime. This is legal but it is not ethical because a confessed criminal should pay for his crimes.

On the negotiation table, bluffing is accepted, but a number of negotiators consider it unethical.

4. **Maintain your ethics at all times**

   You should be aware of your actions during the negotiation process. It can be wearisome to negotiate while remaining ethical - but it could be done. The following are tips on how to remain ethical all throughout the activity:

   - **Be honest**

     Be honest. Don't deliberately lie or mislead your co-negotiators. If they come to learn that you can be trusted, negotiating with them the second time around will be easy. Acquire the ability of being able to empathize with other people. Through this manner, you can understand their position.

   - **Learn how to say "no"**

     Have the courage to say "no" when you think that the proposal is unethical or not acceptable. Apparently, you have to back up your refusal with a valid reason. Look at the other party straight in the eye and say "no".

   - **Keep your word**

By keeping your word, people will come to trust you and your reputation will grow as a reliable negotiator. So, don't promise anything if you cannot fulfill your promises. This is one of the purposes of preparing your plans before participating in the negotiations. Know what you can actually offer on the table and how far you are allowed to negotiate.

- **Observe the Ground Rules and be aware of the law**

    Go over the Ground Rules and ascertain you implement them. Be cognizant of the law that is applicable in your particular state as well. Remember that 'ignorance of the law excuses no one.'

- **Be brave to walk away when the terms are unacceptable**

    A superb negotiator can walk away without qualms when the outcome of the negotiation is unacceptable. You may not realize it but the best deals are those that you have turned down because they don't conform to your ethical standards, values, and objectives. This courageous stance will permit you to obtain the best results from any of your negotiations.

Remaining ethical during negotiations will bolster your reputation and people will trust and respect you.

Chapter 11: Negotiating with Your Boss

One of the most difficult negotiations is negotiating with your boss. Your boss holds a higher position than you do; he's your employer who is responsible in putting food on your table. This can intimidate you and let you cower in fear. What more, if you get on the wrong footing with him, he may fire you. Hence, when negotiating with your boss, be tactful and professional. You will have to do it properly to succeed. You may want to follow these steps:

Step #1 – Be sure about what you want to negotiate

Before deciding to negotiate, make sure you have a valid justification to do it. You have to prepare comprehensively about what you want to negotiate. What will your boss get out of your offer? Take note that your boss must also get something out of it. You will have to consider his/her personality when preparing your arguments.

Let's say you want to negotiate for a raise, you will have to research about relevant data, such as:

- Common minimum wage for personnel in your category.
- Benefits enjoyed by various individuals in the same rank as yours
- Minimum wage required by law in your specific state or area
- Hours of duty
- Your benefits granted by your boss
- Your job specifications
- Job specifications of other workers with the same position in different companies
- How your boss and the company can benefit from your offer

- Justification of why you are asking for a raise

Based on the above-mentioned facts, prepare your talking points. Prioritize which statement should come first. You may want to write down your arguments and bring the summary with you during the negotiation. Memorize your first statements because one tends to be nervous during opening statements. This will allow you to gather your wits and gain self-confidence.

Step #2 – Choose the correct timing

You may be well-prepared but your timing is off. You cannot ask for a raise at the end of the year when everyone is busy writing reports and evaluations of events done during the year. The ideal time to ask for a raise is when the personnel assessments are done, usually before the next year commences.

If you have received an excellent performance, you can use this as your primary focus in requesting for a salary adjustment. Ascertain that your boss is also in a good mood and has sufficient time to listen. In addition, ask yourself if the company can afford to increase your salary. Perhaps, the company is in a slump and could not give in to your demands. If that is the case, you will have to wait for a more opportune time.

It's preferable that you inform your boss of your plan beforehand, so he can adjust his schedule accordingly. Surprise meetings are not always welcomed, especially in a busy workplace.

Step #3 – Present your case

Prepare your presentation in such a way that the goals of your employer is in conjunction with your goals. Don't allow your emotions to control you, but present the concrete facts to support your request. These facts should be well-documented and noted. Prepare two hard copies, so you can leave the second copy with your boss.

You can present your arguments/case using a PowerPoint slide presentation. This will help you present your focal points more clearly. You can highlight items you want to emphasize.

Speak clearly and confidently. Be straightforward but polite. Before your meeting, you can perform the breathing exercises presented in chapter 3 to ease your nervousness.

Your ACOA (Alternative Course of Action) must be ready in case your first proposal is rejected.

Listen carefully to any questions or recommendations from your boss. Answer the questions honestly and take note of the recommendations.

Step #4 - Work on a compromise

If your first proposal is not accepted, you should negotiate with your boss and work on a compromise. Don't walk away. Discuss with him your ACOA. Be ready to adjust your proposals and accommodate some of his suggestions. Bear in mind that a negotiation indicates collaboration. So, be willing to work with him on an acceptable term for both of you.

Step #5 - Document the final agreement

You must document what transpired during the negotiation. This can be signed by both of you. This will serve as a temporary proof of what you have agreed on, while the formal document is still being prepared.

Step #6 – Shake hands

After the negotiation, shake hands with your boss and thank him for taking time out from his busy schedule to accommodate your request. Observing good manners and right conduct, AFTER you have achieved what you wanted will put you in a good light.

Asking for a raise needs coordination and extensive preparation. Be prepared for that.

Chapter 12: Negotiating with a Business Partner

At some point in your life, you may have to negotiate with a potential business partner. The same pointers apply to this win-win type of negotiation. Take note, since you will be using the win-win approach, your strategy will have to be non-confrontational. You will have to look out for your partner's welfare too. To help you out in negotiating with your business partner, here are suggested steps that you can implement:

Step #1 – Prepare for the negotiation

Like all the first steps in a negotiation, you have to do your homework. Research about the business and all its related aspects. You may want to research about your intended business partner too. You wouldn't want a shady character as your partner, right? Inform him of the ground rules that you have created. Refer to chapter 4 for the creation of ground rules.

Step #2 – Set your own objectives

Prepare your primary and sub goals. You can create an educated guess about what your business partner may want as well. They must be in congruence with your own objectives.

Step #3 – Give him time to discuss his expectations from the partnership

What does he expect to gain from your partnership? You can ask questions to clarify whatever doubts you have. What are his goals? How would the revenues be split between the two of you? How much ROI (Return of Investment) does he expect after a year? What can he contribute to the partnership? How much would be his initial investment? Ask all pertinent questions during the negotiations. A set of common questions should be answered by both of you.

Step #4 – Present your own business platform

In this type of negotiation, being honest is critical. You are business partners after all. Explain to him your own proposal. Avoid misleading or undermining him.

Step #5 – Discuss the merits of each proposal

Discuss what items should be included in your agreement. You will be sorting out the most essential items from both of your proposals to prepare the contract for your business partnership. Because it's a partnership the benefit will have to be distributed evenly between the two of you.

Step #6 – Prepare a formal document

The outcome of the negotiation must be written in black and white and documented properly. In cases, when the negotiation is not completed, the minutes of your meeting should still be documented and signed. The formal document can be processed after everything is finalized.

Step #7 – Part ways with a warm handshake

A warm handshake can seal a fruitful negotiation. This indicates that you are looking forward to the partnership.

Step #8 – Implement the agreement

Ensure that you have done your part conscientiously in implementing the conditions in the contract. It's for your own self-interest. The success of your business will depend on how trustworthy and hardworking you are. So, perform your part of the bargain and your business will prosper.

These are the main steps in negotiating with a prospective business partner. You can utilize the other steps in the different negotiation methods when needed.

Chapter 13: Negotiating with Multiple Groups

Most of the time negotiations take place between two persons or two parties. Nevertheless, there will come a time that you may be called on to participate in negotiations with multiple groups. In this type of negotiation, there are additional tasks that have to be done. Let's assume you are in charge of this negotiation, here are things you have to do:

1. In the same manner that you have conducted the two-party negotiations, you must follow the basic steps too.

2. Make sure that everyone has been notified of the place, time, and day of the negotiation.

3. Each participant must have received a copy of the ground rules and has signed an acknowledgment of that fact.

4. Each negotiator must have an assigned role to perform during the negotiation.

5. Before the negotiation proper, each participant has to introduce himself/herself to make the ambiance less formal.

6. The seating arrangement has to allow all negotiators to be able to look at each other.

7. Meet each group and get to know them before the negotiation, and explain what is expected from them. You may want to reiterate that they should read the ground rules because you may be amiable but you will not tolerate unprofessional conduct.

8. Establish order as early as possible. Let them know who is in control. Be helpful as much as possible though. This will show them that you want to reduce their anxiety, so that negotiations will not be strained.

9. Having lots of participants mean that there will be multiple ideas, concepts and bargaining chips on the table. Be ready to mediate during power struggles.

10. Watch out for volatile situations. You have to know how to defuse the situation when this happens.

11. Ask them questions and listen intently to their answers. What are their goals and thoughts about the negotiation? Derive your judgment from their responses. But suspend your judgment when your information is incomplete.

12. Being able to identify their personalities will help you in monitoring them, and surmising who can be tough or easy to convince to your side.

13. Multiple parties can be problematic when activities are disorganized. Hence, you have to let them police their ranks. Assign a leader for each group. The leader will help you maintain order during the negotiation.

Steps in negotiating with multiple parties

Step #1 – Learn about each party

Aside from knowing about the negotiation, acquire all information about each party. Meet them before the actual negotiation, so you can get to know them better.

Step #2 – Justify and support your stand

Present your proposal and justify and support it. Encourage them to ask questions, so you can explain to them your position.

Step #3 – Allow them to present their proposal

Ask pertinent questions too to clarify and discern more why they have chosen their stand. Ask them what their objectives are and what they intent to achieve.

Step #4 – Work with them to solve the problem

Many heads are better than one, so discuss how you can resolve the conflicting issues. Brainstorm on how you can arrive at a compromise. With the cooperation of everyone, you will definitely come to a conclusion.

Step #5 – Finalize your contract

Finalize the contract that you have agreed on. Prepare the contract and have it duly signed by all parties.

Step #6 – Implement the contract

You can now implement the contract. The implementation will have to be monitored, to ensure that everything is in order, and the terms in the contract are followed.

The steps are similar - only there are more tasks to complete.

Chapter 14: Negotiating with Your Kids

Negotiating with your kids is not a walk in the park. It can be a tough task, even if you're their parent. This is the reason why some parents exercise their authority over their children instead of negotiating with them. This is not a recommended parenting method, however, because it prevents kids from learning how to deal with conflicts. Your kids must learn how to negotiate skillfully in order to survive this highly competitive era.

Learning this skill from an early age will help them succeed in their daily dealings with people around them. But parents should remember that there is a time to negotiate and a time NOT to negotiate.

An example is when your kid wants to stay overnight with her friends, who are suspected of drug addiction. This is not a case that can be negotiated. There is no room for a negotiation. As a parent, you have to step in and enforce your authority to prevent her from going.

You can allow your children to negotiate in other cases, such as negotiating for their playtime, or how they can spend their weekends more productively.

Here are pointers you can implement when negotiating with your kids:

1. **Be flexible with your older kids**

    You can rationalize with older kids, so you can be more flexible when negotiating with them. Appeal to their sense of responsibility.

2. **Give them the freedom to present their arguments**

When you allow your kids to present their arguments, you are teaching them how to solve conflicts in a constructive manner. When their suggestions are recognized, they are inclined to participate more actively because the ideas came from them. Allow them to choose their preferred option.

3. Be clear with your expectations

Before the event, state your expectations clearly. Each child must understand what your objective is. An example is when you are out to buy new toys and you want to cut on cost. You can say:

> "I know, you all want to by new toys but we have to skimp because of our summer vacation next week. What about limiting your purchase to only one toy?"

Some of your kids may argue that they want at least two toys. So, you can concede, on one condition that the price of the two toys should not exceed $30.

4. Create a win-win situation

The example above is a win-win situation, where you and your kids are happy with the result. Your kids can learn also that they can compromise.

5. Respect your kids

Show them that you respect their ideas. Listen to them and decide whether the case is negotiable or not. Either way, you have to explain why. Do this in a calm and reassuring voice. Never shout or lose your cool in front of them.

6. Be firm when you don't want to negotiate

When the case is non-negotiable, state firmly your position and establish your authority at the onset. Examples are:

> *"Time to go to bed dearies, but no one goes to bed with dirty feet."*

> *"Breakfast is ready, but only for those who have brushed their teeth."*

7. Adjust your negotiating style according to your kids' ages

Negotiating with a tot is different from negotiating with a teen. For young children, you can present good alternatives that they can select from. For teens, you can allow them to suggest the alternatives themselves and then you discuss to select the best choice for you and your kid. As you practice negotiating with your kids, you will eventually get the hang of it. You will learn too what works for each of your children.

8. Treat them with love

Anything that you do must be done with love. Love is a universal language that can move mountains. No matter how the negotiations proceed, show your kids that you love them.

Some parents expressed their concern about allowing kids to negotiate; saying that the kids are given power and authority, which they can abuse. This can happen when the parent doesn't know how to maintain his authority. The children can be given choices and have control over their choices but the primary authority will always lie with the parents.

Steps in negotiating with your kids

Step #1 – Explain your goal/s

Explain your goal to your kids and answer whatever questions they have. The goal or objective must be stated clearly. Examples of goals are:

- "To reduce monthly living expenses by $500."
- "To open a bank account for each child, with each child depositing $40 a month." (The money will come from their savings from their daily allowance.)
- "Every day, each child will have to do the specified household chore assigned to him.

The objectives are not ambiguous but are specific. You will be able to monitor easily whether the goals are accomplished or not.

Discuss the purpose of reducing your monthly living expenses by $500; why they have to save and why they have to help with the household chores.

Step #2 – Listen to their thoughts

After you have stated your proposal, it's time to listen to your kids. Let them argue their points. Try to understand their point of view. Assist them on their plan of action by discussing how they can obtain their goals. An example is how to reduce their living expenses. This is the step where they are allowed to bargain and plead their 'cause'.

Step #3 – Brainstorm with your kids on how you can achieve your goals

This is the step where your kids can bargain with you to solve the problem. You can present options for your kids to choose from. The most recommended method is to let them formulate the options among themselves. This will prompt them to participate actively in attaining their goals. Ascribe the idea as theirs, so they can take full responsibility for its implementation.

Step #4 – Provide guidance on problems they may encounter

Support their plans and provide guidance when needed. You are still their parent and their guiding light. So, learn how to balance when to give them the authority and when not to. You can refer to more about this topic in the previous chapters.

Step #5 – Conclude the negotiations and implement the agreement

To create a more formal atmosphere and demonstrate to your children that you mean business, you can motivate them to sign an agreement form. It is recommended that you prepare a compliance form or a log book too, where they can put a check mark of the assigned task that they have done for the day. Through this, you can monitor conveniently the progress of their goals.

Step #6 – Appreciate their efforts

You should express your appreciation for their effort in assisting you with your objectives. Tell them how they have performed well in the negotiations. This will boost their self-confidence in participating in future negotiations.

Kids are quick learners and with your able guidance, they can become effective negotiators in the future.

Chapter 15: Controlling Your Emotions

Emotions play an essential role on how you behave during negotiations. These can become evident in the way you act and conduct yourself. During negotiations, you must learn how to control your emotions. This is because you cannot negotiate effectively if you're too emotional or angry. The other party will know all your thoughts before you can even utter a word, just by looking at your face. Thus, you have to be poker-faced when negotiating.

Negative emotions, such as anger, frustration, anxiety and depression can definitely affect the negotiation negatively. Many inexperienced negotiators think that anger can help extract their goals from the other party, but this is untrue. The goals may have been achieved but in the long run, the negative effect will soon emerge.

How can you control your emotions, or that of your counterpart?

You can control your emotions by doing the following:

1. **Take a step away**

    When you are consumed by anger or anxiety, take a step away and distance yourself for a few minutes from the activity. However, don't worry, a little anxiety is normal.

2. **Perform breathing or calming exercises before the negotiations**

    Perform the breathing exercises, while relaxing, as presented in chapter 3. These will help calm your nerves and reduce your anxiety.

3. **Practice in front of a mirror**

Look at yourself in the mirror and try smiling. Practice smiling without showing any negative emotions. Psyching yourself daily will prod your subconscious. Soon, you will be smiling without making an effort.

4. **Psyche yourself**

   Psyche yourself mentally through auto-suggestion. *"I'm calm and relaxed; I can succeed."* You can repeat this statement mentally until your subconscious recognizes it.

5. **Control your mannerisms**

   Avoid fidgeting, playing with your hair, or popping your knuckles. Mannerisms denote that you are nervous, and they undermine your credibility as a self-confident and well-prepared negotiator.

6. **Reframe your thoughts**

   When your emotions become ugly and negative, it's time you reframe your thoughts. Think about positive things that made you happy. Focus on these positive thoughts until you are relieved.

You can control the emotions of the other party by:

1. **Not reacting to them**

   If the other party explodes in anger, don't respond. Remain calm and collected. Give him time to recover by taking a break.

2. **Ignore negative emotions and focus on the positive emotions**

Do not nitpick. Leave the negative emotions and acknowledge the positive ones. "Your idea of split earnings is commendable. Let's discuss how we can do that."

The statement draws the focus away from the anger, and points out what must be done, instead.

3. **Act in a manner that prevents the person to become emotional**

    Stay away from the topic that made the person emotional. You can always go back when the person has regained his composure.

Emotions when expressed positively will benefit you and the other party. So harness your emotions properly.

Chapter 16: Handling Problems during Negotiations

Problems are bound to arise during dynamic processes, such as negotiations. For you to proceed unhampered, you will have to handle these problems responsibly. How would you handle these problems?

1. **Intent to 'destroy' the other party**

    You can detect immediately a negotiator who is out to destroy the other party through his verbal and nonverbal language. This is one of the tactics of ruthless negotiators who want to gain an advantage at the expense of the other party.

    When this happens, and you're at the receiving end, quit the negotiations. There's no reason why you should stay and tolerate the abuses. You can find more responsible people to negotiate with. Before leaving the table, be certain you have informed the other party about the reason of your refusal to continue with the negotiations.

2. **Emotional outbursts**

    During an emotional outburst by any of the participants, you must maintain your composure and act as the mediator. Request for a break, then talk to the person involved. Resolve the issue by reminding him/her that the ground rules specify that emotional outbursts are not allowed. A warning is given to the person. The next violation will mean the person's removal from the negotiation table.

3. **Objections that are too personal, hostile and irrelevant**

   Negotiators who ask irrelevant questions, act hostile and focus on personal matters are given a warning for the first offense, then termination on the second offense.

4. **Combative and rude behavior**

   Rudeness should not be tolerated during negotiations. Likewise, negotiators with a belligerent attitude must be given a warning. These bad behaviors can disrupt the organized procedure of negotiations.

5. **Non-compliance to ground rules**

   A few scalawags may intentionally ignore the ground rules during negotiations. This happens most of the time with bad faith and adversarial negotiations. You will have to enforce the sanction for non-compliance. This is the reason why you have to establish first the ground rules before the start of the negotiations. All participants in the negotiations must have a copy with the receipt duly signed by the receiver.

6. **Misrepresentation of facts**

   Deliberate distortion or misrepresentation of facts must be dealt more severely because this could render the contract null and void. Termination from the negotiation is recommended with this type of problem.

For the rest of the problems, the sanctions should rely on the ground rules created for the negotiation. Having ground rules that are specific and in detail will help you cope with the behavioral problems occurring during your negotiations.

Chapter 17: Examples of Negotiation Conversations

Negotiation conversations are included in this book because lots of readers are searching for conversation samples that they can refer to. Go over these conversation examples and use them if they apply to your situation. The background process is not discussed in this chapter because this has been discussed in the previous chapter. Here are the recommended conversations. Use them to your heart's content.

Negotiating for a raise with your boss

You: *"Good morning sir, I have come for my appointment."*

Boss: *"Right, have a seat."*

You: *"Thank you."*

Boss: *"So, why do you need a raise?"*

You: *"I have grown professionally in the past two years based on the awards that I was accorded."* (Show certificates of awards)

"I have also worked conscientiously for the company even beyond working hours." (Show record of perfect attendance)

"I have spearheaded the company's outreach programs for indigent individuals." (Show program and list of activities done)

"My performance rating is 96%, and I have performed more than what my job specifications stipulate."

Boss: *"Okay, so your performance is commendable but the company has not yet promoted staff members that had worked for only 2 years or less."*

You: *"But sir, I have researched on the salary scheme of employees who have the same designation as me, and my salary is way below the mark."* (Show list).

*"Also, I went over the government approved minimum wage for people in my position and mine is not up to par." (*Show printout of legislative law*)*

Boss: *"So, what are your figures? Don't rejoice yet. I will have to consult the higher ups for your case.*

You: *"I would like to adopt the government's approved minimum wage."*

Boss: *"I'll see what I can do."*

You: *"Thank you, sir. I appreciate your taking time to listen to my request."*

Negotiating for the price of a second-had car with a sales agent

Sales agent: *"Welcome Ma'am, may I help you?"*

You: *"I would like to buy a used car."*

Sales agent: *"Do you have any preferences?"*

You: *"I prefer a Ford GT coupe, please."*

Sales agent: *"We have a Ford GT here but it's the 2006 model. Anyway, it has the same basic features."*

You: *"Let me see."*

Sales agent: *"This car has been used for only 6 months. Look at the mileage; it's only 574 mi. The price is only $74,560."*

You: *"I don't like the color of the upholstery; I will have to change it. That would be an additional expenditure for me. What about $50,000?"*

Sales agent: *"Are you kidding me? Ma'am, that's way too cheap."*

You: *"Then, let's settle for $60,000. I will have to bring this to my personal mechanic for an overhaul. Look at the fender, it got scratches."*

Sales agent: *"$72. The engine is working smoothly and that's what's important."*

You: *"Well, for me, every aspect must be considered. I have researched, and $72 is way too expensive. $63.'*

Sales agent: *"$70."*

You: *"$64."*

Sales agent: *"$69."*

You: *"$65. Take it or leave it."*

You will have to walk away, if he doesn't agree because you have issued an ultimatum.

Sales agent: *"I'm sorry Ma'am, but that's not acceptable."*

You: *"Oh, okay. I will have to look elsewhere. Thank you for your assistance."*

The sales agent will run after you, if he deems your offer reasonable. If not, then you can always go back to purchase it, after doing the rounds of car shops and comparing prices and features.

Negotiating with your child about his sleeping hours:

You: "*Let's sit down. I have something important to tell you.*"

Child: "*Okay, dad.*"

You: "*Do you want to grow as tall as dad?*"

Child: "*Yup.*"

You: "*Then you have to sleep as much as you can.*"

Child: "*How can sleep help me grow?*"

You: "*It's when you're sleeping that the growth molecules come out and build your bones and muscles.*"

Child: "*Really? No kidding?*"

You: "*No kidding.*"

Child: "*But I have enough sleep during night time.*"

You: "*You need at least 10 to 12 hours of sleep per day to allow the growth molecules to function well.*

Child: "*U-huh.*"

You: "*So, you will have to use some of your play time to be able to sleep 10 hours.*"

Child: "*How many hours would that be?*"

You: "*around 1 to 2 hours.*"

Child: "*Then, can I play anytime I want during weekends?*"

You: *"Alright, but every day, you should take a 1 to 2-hour nap during the day, and then go to sleep early at around 7:30 pm."*

Child: *"Sure, Dad."*

You: *"Thank you sweetie for being so cooperative. Love you."*

These are sample conversations that you can pattern yours from. Every case is distinctive, so adjust the script to suit your conversational style. Keep in mind that you should be aggressive but not combative.

Chapter 18: Expressions/Statements that Excellent Negotiators Use

As you become skilled in negotiating, your vocabulary would change to acquire more suitable language for this activity. The following are examples of statements that you can use as a negotiator:

1. "I can understand your point of view, however…,"
2. "Your proposal is relevant, but…,"
3. "It's great that you're concerned about the welfare of the buyers, however…,"
4. "Kindly justify why you have chosen that stance?"
5. "You have stated your objective clearly, but…,"
6. "That was a superb presentation. Thank you."
7. "Thank you for clarifying your position."
8. "Please expound further."
9. "I had a wonderful time collaborating with you."
10. "I look forward to a productive business relationship with you."
11. "I feel for you, and we will look into your concern. In the meantime…"
12. "That's a sound suggestion. Let me just…"

What you should NOT say as a negotiator:

1. "You're wasting my time."
2. "I don't have time for this."
3. "You're so immature."
4. "You're uncouth."
5. "Shut up!"
6. "Get out of the room."
7. "I don't want to listen to your litany of miseries."
8. "Is there someone else, other than you, whom I can deal with?"
9. "You're spewing nonsense."
10. "I'm done with you."

11. "This is trash!"
12. "You're a liar."

Instead of saying:

"Shut up!"

You can say:

"Let's give the floor to other participants."

Or:

"Let's stick to the time limit allotted for speaking. May I now present my proposal?"

People are naturally conscious of their self-esteem and how others perceive them. Thus, they don't want to be embarrassed publicly. Watch your words during negotiations because you may unintentionally hurt someone by your pronouncements.

Use positive words when negotiating. Positive words will foster a positive environment where both parties can be relaxed and happy.

Examples of some positive words are:

- Cooperation
- Collaboration
- Common good
- Common goals
- Beneficial
- Compromise
- Contract
- Camaraderie
- Trust
- Honesty
- Loyal

- Agreement

Awareness of the decency of your language will affect your negotiations. Make sure you use the proper language; use it at the right time and use it with the proper tone off voice.

Chapter 19: Handling Objections in Negotiations

Objections will most likely occur during negotiations. This is because people with conflicting ideas come together to discuss a solution to their problems. Objections can be valid, however.

As a buyer-seller negotiator, you will have to determine if the objections are worth a second glance. How can you do this? This is done by viewing the validity of the objections.

Let's say the objection was about the expensive price of your product. Let's assume that you are the seller. As a seller, you should never agree with the objections of the buyer. You have to prepare beforehand and foresee possible objections to your product. Afterwards, you find an answer to the objections. During the negotiation, you will have face the objections and answer them.

As with the example above, you can reply by saying that the material used for your product is of high quality that is why it's more expensive.

After the negotiation, you may want to conduct a research on the prices of the same product in the market. The result will prove if your product is indeed, overpriced or not.

Knowing your product well will help you defend it from objections.

Other types of objections are:

- Objection to the delivery of the product
- Objection to the product material
- Objection to the buyer
- Objection to the style of the product
- Objection to the time of purchase
- Objection to the source of the material

- Objection to their need of the product

Here are specific strategies in handling these objections:

1. **Pre-empting**

    This is a method in which you handle the objections before they happen. You can do this by examining your product and then projecting what buyers will object to. Find the answers to these objections, so that when objected to, you have a ready answer.

    This can only be done if you know your product well. When you are confident about your product, you will be able to handle all the objections easily. It is in this context that you should only promote or sell products that are durable and reliable.

2. **Deflection**

    You avoid or deflect the objection and just allow it to pass. Pretend the objection never happened. This is applicable when the buyer is not truly interested in your product.

3. **Humor**

    Respond by cracking a joke. If you can do this, then you should be lauded. Humor can positively break the ice, but not everyone can recount a good joke.

4. **Justification**

    You acknowledge the objection as valid and justified. But it is your product and you believe it's still the best in the market.

5. **LAIR: Listen, Acknowledge, Identify objection, Reverse it**

   This method means that you will listen to their objections, acknowledge them, identify what the objection is all about and then reverse it. This is done by explaining to the buyer that the reverse of his objection is the fact that is actually true.

   In the example above (too expensive price), it can be reversed when you explain that your product is in fact cheaper, in the long run, because the material used is expensive but durable. The product can be used for several years and will save money for the buyer.

   On the other hand the cheaper brand is actually more expensive because the buyer will have to buy frequently. This is because the cheaper product is not durable and is easily destroyed. Eventually, the buyer will be spending more. He has to buy three of the cheaper product against one of the initially more expensive product.

   As a negotiator, you have to be on your toes to reason out and defend your product.

6. **Boomerang**

   You return or bounce back their objections. If they say your product is expensive, you can explain in the same manner as #5 – your product is cheaper - in the long run.

7. **Pushback**

   You may also object to the buyer's objection by expressing your objection. "That's not fair. You should look at the whole picture. I object to your objection." This means that the objection does not affect the durability of the product.

8. Tipping the bucket

You ask the buyer to reveal all his objections. Once these are revealed, you can then help to resolve them. This will show to the buyer that you truly care for them, and he will begin to trust you. When trust is established, the objections can be reframed or renamed, and the product becomes acceptable to the buyer.

9. Reframing

The objection is reframed by altering the buyer's cognitive frame. Once this is done, the objection can become re-categorized. The buyer will perceive the product in a different frame of mind.

10. Renaming

You can also change the name so that the meaning becomes different. Once the objection is renamed, it would be easier to handle.

11. Objection writing

You can write down the objections and then crossing them out. This means that the objection has been resolved.

These objections can sometimes be viewed as obstacles but to a wise negotiator, these objections can be turned the other way around. People will constantly raise objections even with products that they need. They do this to secure a better deal (lower price) from the sellers. Still, a smart seller would not fall into this trap. Using the methods above; you can continually devise ways and means to give the buyer a better deal without creating a mountain out of the mole hills of objections.

Chapter 20: Tips to Remember When Negotiating

Negotiating effectively is a challenging endeavor. You need all the assistance you can muster. To help you with the process, here are valuable tips that you can use.

1. **Always be ready for your negotiations**. NEVER negotiate without full knowledge about what the negotiation is all about. Again, knowledge is power. Research, research and research. Preparation is a crucial aspect of negotiations. It could mean the failure or success of your activity.

2. **Prepare the main objective and the ACOA beforehand.** You must have not only one major proposal but several alternative ones.

3. **Be ethical.** As discussed in early chapters, negotiate ethically. Your ethical performance will promote your reputation as an outstanding negotiator.

4. **Ascertain that the other party is also satisfied with the deal**. The result should be a win-win agreement. Keep in mind that you may negotiate again with the same group in the future. Hence, ensure that the other party is treated fairly.

5. **Keep an open mind.** Negotiations can vary from one event to another. Be prepared to welcome changes and adjust according to the current situation. Before the negotiation, prepare yourself mentally. The mind is a superb 'machine' that can control the way you behave.

6. **Don't permit a personal issue to affect the outcome of the negotiation**. If you are in bad terms

with the negotiator previously, don't let this affect your well-organized plans. Put aside your enmity and focus on the issue at hand.

7. **Cooperate with the other party to achieve a win-win result**. You may want to help the other group attain their goals, while fulfilling yours. This is possible when both groups realize that it's a cooperative venture and not a competitive activity.

8. **Practice makes perfect.** You can only acquire the skills required for negotiations when you practice them. Practice them daily in your dealings with people around you and will ultimately acquire the skills.

9. **The negotiation should lead to better deals**. If it does not, then the result is unfavorable. You may want to make revisions, while the agreement is not yet implemented, but this will require the consensus of the other party.

10. **Learn from your mistakes.** Nobody is perfect. Give yourself some leeway. Forgive yourself but learn from your mistakes. Your mistakes are the rungs in your stairway to success.

11. **Teach your kids how to negotiate correctly**. By negotiating with your kids, you're already teaching them how to do it. Nonetheless, do not relinquish total control of your authority to your children. Again, there must be a stable balance between what they can negotiate and what they cannot.

12. **Avoid using the win-lose or lose-lose negotiations**. Use them only when absolutely necessary. They are not intended for building social relationships.

13. **Be a good sport.** In cases when you lose a negotiation, show the other party that you are not a sore loser. Shake hands with the other party and get over it. There will be other negotiations that you will conquer.

14. **Smile during negotiations.** Smiling is easier than pouting. This simple action will help ease the tension. It's infectious too. The other party can take the cue and, sooner or later, will smile as well.

15. **Adopt a sense of humor**. Negotiating is a challenging and exhausting endeavor. Therefore, you need to adopt a sense of humor to break the ice and ease exhaustion. Being able to laugh and insert jokes at the right time is a skill that not everyone possesses. Expert negotiators are adept in cracking jokes. You can develop this skill as you participate more in negotiations.

16. **Don't reveal your BATNAS** (best alternative to a negotiated agreement), when presenting the first offer, or even during the course of the negotiations. Some negotiators do not reveal their BATNAS until the negotiation is concluded.

17. **The outcome should be based on an objective standard**. This will erase doubts on the validity of the negotiation. It would also guarantee that your negotiations are above board.

18. **Assist the other party to attain his goals**. A reliable negotiator will ascertain that the other party is happy with the results.

19. **Consider the other negotiators as business friends** that you will deal with in the future. This will motivate you too be considerate and fair with them.

Remember the Golden Rule: "Do unto others what you like others do unto you."

20. **Negotiations are learning experiences**. Hence, participate in them as often as you can. You may want to invite your family members and friends to practice the skill.

Learning how to negotiate properly is a skill that you can acquire from your daily activities. Be conscious of these opportunities, so you can grab them swiftly. Let every negotiation you participate in enhance your skills and broaden your knowledge.

Conclusion

To be able to negotiate effectively and successfully, you may want to implement all the pointers provided in this book. At first, you will find it challenging to negotiate. But with practice, you can become an excellent negotiator.

Acquiring the skills of a splendid negotiator is a pipe dream that many people only dream of. Nonetheless, in your case, you can make this happen. You may not be aware of it, but you are negotiating every day as you deal with other people. Develop your skill in negotiating by practicing at home with your children and family members. Experience is the best teacher and practicing will help you fulfill your dreams.

With all the information provided in this book and with your dedication and commitment, you will certainly succeed.

www.ingramcontent.com/pod-product-compliance
Lightning Source LLC
Chambersburg PA
CBHW061444180526
45170CB00004B/1547